THE LITTLE
FOXES

FOREWORD BY
Dr. Frank Ofosu-Appiah

The Ignored Things
That Fight Harder
than Demons

SONGS OF SOLOMON 2:15

THE LITTLE
FOXES

ERIC FORDJOUR

EQUIP
PUBLISHING
HOUSE

ISBN 978-1-8380507-1-9

EMAIL THE AUTHOR VIA
e.fordjour@cfmuk.org

COVER DESIGN
Bright Osei-Assibey

LAYOUT DESIGN
Bright Amoako-Attah

EDITING
EPH Editorial

Unless otherwise indicated, Scripture quotations are from the New International Version (NIV).

Printed in the United Kingdom.

*I dedicate this book to
my wonderful and supportive wife;
Adelaide Fordjour and my little angels;
Leseley, Declan, Beverley and Ariel.
Guys you made it happen.
Daddy loves you all.*

Contents

Acknowledgements

I would like to thank God for placing the desire and ability in me to birth '*The Little Foxes*'. A big thank you to Dr. Frank Ofosu-Appiah for inspiring me to write this book.

Again, thank you goes to Mr. Richard Ellimah. My brother, you have been there from the beginning to the end. This wouldn't have been possible without your massive help and support. Another thanks goes to Mr. Bright Osei-Assibey the CEO of '9Creations'.

Thank you to all the Pastors and Leaders of CFM.

To my amazing CFM family, guys you have been wonderful and supportive along this journey and all I can say is may God bless you.

Last but not the least, kudos to Equip Publishing House for taking on this project to publish my book. Words are truly not enough to say thank you. Your service is truly excellent.

Foreword

I chanced upon a short write up by Pastor Eric Fordjour on Facebook where he was giving some great advice especially to young ministers. I suddenly found myself going back occasionally to read his latest instalment. In fact, I looked forward to it. His words were a depth of insight and the wisdom was riveting. There were some of them that I found myself saying, "this is too short, please don't stop, we need more of such direct, no holds barred truths". I was hooked!

After a little cajoling and a promise to write the foreword if he put his wise thoughts into a book, here you are with it. This is a little book that carries a big punch. It will challenge many little things that we tend to overlook in life and ministry. Just as big doors swing on little hinges and small keys open big gates, so the little and often ignored things tend to bring us the biggest results.

In this book, Pastor Eric, from the overflow of God's wisdom and experience as a minister of God, draws attention to things that matter most. It is undeniable that the terrain of church life and leadership is littered with many casualties who could and should have made better and lasting impact. The reasons for such implosion are many, but our attention is drawn in this book to some of them that may seem insignificant but so important. It is my prayer that this will be a must read for every young, and even older minister and worker in church.

If you are conversant with the great preacher Charles Spurgeon's book, John Ploughman's Talk, (if not, please get one for yourself), I can say without equivocation that this is our modern day version of it. The advice is practical, wise, applicable, but above all, spiritual. If we will do church, then we must do it right and in a way the honors the Master. His church has suffered in many ways because the custodians have not done their due diligence in manifesting His nature.

The world is constantly changing, values are shifting and positions are evolving. People are confused, they are asking questions in a world where truth is relative. Who is going to take the stand to steer affairs and guide people? I believe it will be those who refuse to compromise and fade into the shadows of pressure and appeasement. Who will be prepared to pay the price of walking the narrow way of love, humility and integrity? Who, like Nehemiah of old, will weep over the broken down walls of Christian ministry? Who will stand and be ready to do the hard work of helping to fix our walls and systems?

Pastor Eric has answered that call and his book is part of the piece that will help fix the broken walls and systems. Young preacher, emerging leader, aspiring prophet, I highly recommend this book to you. Please read it carefully, read it slowly and read it prayerfully. Make notes, and indeed make plenty of it as you reflect on the truths. But above all, endeavor to live out the time-tested truths given and I can assure you the little foxes will have no ability to destroy your vine of ministry and leadership. Creation is waiting on your manifestation of leadership.

Read On!

FRANK OFOSU-APPIAH

Pastor, All Nations Church
Chancellor, Institute Of Leadership and Development (iLEAD)

1
Young Preacher

CHAPTER ONE

Young Preacher

YOUNG PREACHER, LEAD BY EXAMPLE!

TITUS 2:7 (NIV)

'In everything set them an example by doing what is good. In your teaching show integrity, seriousness.'

The people you lead will learn more from your exemplary life than from your preaching. Spend a lot more time being a good example, especially for other young people who want to walk in your footsteps. You achieve nothing by sitting on the fence and issuing instructions. In church, do not be ashamed to be an usher if there is a need for it. Mob the altar, if you have to. Receive first-time visitors, if you should. Get off your high horse and hit the streets, evangelising and winning souls for the Lord, instead of spending precious time preaching about it. Take the lead, and the church members will follow your example! No work should be beneath you. You have been called to serve, and serve by being an example to your followers. Learn from the example of Jesus, who washed His disciples' feet. He did it as an example of love for them. Note that the act of feet washing was reserved for the basest of servants. That is how low our Saviour and Master went in order to become a worthy example for us all.

YOUNG PREACHER, WHAT HAPPENED TO YOUR QUIET TIME?

MARK 1:35

'Very early in the morning, while it was still dark, Jesus got up, left the house and went off to a solitary place, where he prayed.' (NIV)

Being a preacher does not make you immune to the basics of Christian maturity. You will need to still spend time with the Lord each day in prayer and in the study of the Word. This is the best way to grow as a Christian. It is only when you grow and mature in Christ that you can be in the best position to support the growth of other Christians. Young Preacher, do not be too busy that you fail to spend time alone with God to receive nourishment. Quality time spent with God also strengthens you. Do not die of spiritual malnutrition!

YOUNG PREACHER, DON'T BE IN A HURRY TO RUBBISH WHAT YOUR FATHERS HAVE BUILT

PROVERBS 30:11

'There are those who curse their fathers and do not bless their mothers...' (NIV)

One of the key fundamental values you must develop as a young preacher is to submit to your spiritual fathers. Do not despise the man who gives you his pulpit to preach. It takes a man with a big heart who understands mentorship to do this. Remember that it is not easy building a successful ministry. It is a blessing to be taken in by a Spiritual Father under his wings. Submit to him and contribute to maintaining the ministry he has built. Do not go and destroy what he has used years of dedication to God, and personal integrity to build. It is the height of wickedness and spiritual immaturity to seek to obliterate what your spiritual father has taken years to build. Do not force yourself to win the congregation's affection in order to destroy your Father in the process!

YOUNG PREACHER, AN EMPIRE CANNOT BE BUILT WITHIN AN EMPIRE

1 CORINTHIANS 3:17

'If anyone destroys God's temple, God will destroy that person; for God's temple is sacred, and you together are that temple.' (NLT)

While serving under your spiritual father, give him your all. Do not be ashamed to serve him. Remember, even though the prophet Elisha knew he had a ministry, he still served his father, the prophet Elijah. He did not go around with shoulders high, bragging and telling everybody he was a better preacher.

A young freshly-graduated preacher who had the prophetic gift was given the opportunity to do a one-week prophetic programme with his church. His spiritual father had travelled out of the country. This young man, on the first day of the programme, stood up and poured scorn on everything his spiritual father had done. He went further and bragged about his spiritual gift, and mocked his spiritual father for his 'inability to see'. He virtually succeeded in building a cult following in that church. By this attitude, this young preacher succeeded in truncating his own otherwise promising ministry. If you know that God has called you to have your own ministry, serve faithfully under your spiritual father, learn the ropes and then when you feel your time is up, have a friendly conversation with him. Ensure that you secure his blessing before you leave. It is a curse to leave in rancour.

YOUNG PREACHER, STOP TRYING TO ALWAYS PROVE A POINT

PROVERBS 12:15

'The way of fools seems right to them, but the wise listen to advice.' (NIV)

One killer of young ministries is the urge to always be right. This attitude is born out of arrogance and self-conceit. Present the Word of God as it is, and leave the Holy Spirit to do the convicting. Do not waste your time trying to prove anything. You are not a rock star or sports icon. You are a servant of God. The task of proving a point is beyond you!

YOUNG PREACHER, WHO ARE YOU TRYING TO PLEASE?

ROMANS 12:2

'Do not be conformed to this world, but be transformed by the renewal of your mind, that by testing you may discern what is the will of God, what is good and acceptable and perfect.' (ESV)

In a self-centred world, everyone is trying to please people and prove that they are the best. Unfortunately, this canker has hit the church much harder. Preachers are out-competing one another, just because they want to please the crowd. Young Preacher, listen. You are only in ministry to please the One who called you: God. No matter how unpalatable the message is that the Lord sends you to deliver, go ahead and deliver it. People may not like it but that is none of your business. People may be uncomfortable with your Christian life. So long as your prime motive is to please the Lord, ignore the crowd's reaction. In delivering your message, or living your life, cut out the theatrics and focus on what is relevant. It is better to please the Lord and be rewarded than to please man and suffer eternal condemnation.

YOUNG PREACHER, REAL MINISTRY CONSISTS OF MORE THAN JUST STANDING IN THE PULPIT

MATTHEW 18:3

'And He said: "Truly I tell you, unless you change and become like little children, you will never enter the kingdom of heaven."' (NIV)

There is more to ministry than standing in the pulpit every Sunday and midweek to preach. In fact, preaching is the least of the activities of ministry. View ministry as a holistic process. If you feel led to usher sometimes, go ahead and do it. Join the evangelism team and go out to the fields where the souls are. When it becomes necessary, take the broom and sweep the church compound. Mop the altar, if you have to. No task in the church should be too lowly for you. Everyone else can abandon church work, but not you. So, look beyond the church. If the supporting ministries are not functioning your preaching becomes meaningless.

YOUNG PREACHER, DON'T THINK YOU KNOW IT ALL

PROVERBS 28:26

'Those who trust in themselves are fools but those who walk in wisdom are kept safe.' (NLT)

1 CORINTHIANS 8:2

'Those who think they know something do not yet know as they ought to know.' (NIV)

Humility to acknowledge that you do not know it all is critical for success in ministry. As a young preacher, you must develop the capacity for knowledge. Be constantly learning. Do not think that you know it all. There is still so much to learn about ministry, about life, about human behaviour, etc. This requires that you consult widely. Talk to your senior minister. Talk to professionals in the church. For instance, if your message has a legal component, talk to a lawyer to understand the full picture before you mount the platform. If it requires some medical knowledge, talk to a health professional and understand things better. Learn in humility!

YOUNG PREACHER, BE OPEN-MINDED BUT DON'T LET YOUR BRAINS FALL OUT

ROMANS 12:2

'Do not copy the behavior and customs of this world, but let God transform you into a new person by changing the way you think. Then you will learn to know God's will for you, which is good and pleasing and perfect.' (NLT)

Young Preacher, do not put yourself into a pigeonhole. Be as open-minded as possible. Understand things outside your domain. Understand people. Understand why people do the things they do. Being open-minded helps you to appreciate situations better, and offer the necessary responses.

YOUNG PREACHER, SOULS ARE PERISHING AND YOU ARE BUSY ARGUING ABOUT IRRELEVANT DOCTRINAL ISSUES

1 TIMOTHY 1:4

'Nor to devote themselves to myths and endless genealogies. These promote controversies rather than God's work-which is by faith.' (NIV)

2 TIMOTHY 2:23

'Don't have anything to do with foolish and stupid arguments, because you know they produce quarrels.' (NIV)

TITUS 3:9

'But avoid foolish controversies and genealogies and arguments and quarrels about the law, because these are unprofitable and useless.' (NIV)

The Apostle Paul admonished his son Timothy to avoid 'fables and endless genealogies'. Such debates will sap your energy, and cause you to deviate from your core duties as a minister of the gospel. Do not let doctrinal debates stand in the way of your primary responsibility of drawing souls into the Kingdom. Listening to some messages being preached on radio and television these days, one gets the impression that some young preachers of today are more interested in defending their doctrinal positions than in preaching the good news of the Kingdom of God. This is a slippery slope you must avoid as a young preacher.

YOUNG PREACHER, DON'T RUSH TO BE A FATHER

JAMES 3:1

'Don't be in any rush to become a teacher, my friends. Teaching is highly responsible work. Teachers are held to the strictest standards.'

(MSG)

These days every man called into ministry wants to be called 'Daddy' or 'Papa'. People use these titles oblivious of the huge responsibilities that go with it. A 'Daddy' or 'Papa' is usually someone who has cut their teeth in ministry; has endured the vicissitudes of life. Daddies and Papas usually have scars to show. They are men of integrity who have served in the vineyard for years. A man does not suddenly get catapulted to the status of a Papa or Daddy. Young Preacher, do not be in a rush to be a Papa or Daddy. You still need mentoring yourself!

YOUNG PREACHER, DON'T SURROUND YOURSELF WITH 'YESSA, MASSA' PEOPLE

PROVERBS 13:20

'Whoever walks with the wise becomes wise, but the companion of fools will suffer harm.' (ESV)

PROVERBS 11:14

'Where there is no guidance, a people falls, but in an abundance of counselors there is safety.' (ESV)

In 1 Kings 12:8-15, we read how the Kingdom of Israel was divided after the death of King Solomon. His son, King Rehoboam faced certain rebellion from his people due to worsening economic conditions. When they sent a delegation to talk to him to reduce the people's burden, he set aside the godly counsel of the wise elders, and rather stuck with the destructive advice of his 'boys' boys'. This act of the king led to the division of the Kingdom of Israel into two. Young Preacher, if you want to go far in ministry, it will depend on your ability to receive godly counsel from people who will be truthful and honest with you.

YOUNG PREACHER, IT'S GOOD TO BRAND YOURSELF BUT DON'T LET THAT TAKE THE CENTRE STAGE OF YOUR MINISTRY

GALATIANS 5:16

'So I say, walk by the Spirit, and you will not gratify the desires of the flesh.' (NIV)

ROMANS 8:5

'Those who live according to the flesh have their minds set on what the flesh desires; but those who live in accordance with the Spirit have their minds set on what the Spirit desires.' (NIV)

It is fashionable for young preachers to brand themselves well. We are increasingly seeing very attractive electronic posters of pastors and the programmes that they do. It is good. But that should not let you lose focus on your core ministry and the One who called you. Whatever form of branding you do should project the Lord, not yourself.

In projecting your gifts, give God the glory. In projecting your church, give the glory to God. In branding your programmes, project God. You cannot brand yourself better than the Lord Jesus Christ, whose servant you are.

YOUNG PREACHER, DON'T DESTROY YOUR REPUTATION BY ASKING EVERYONE YOU COME ACROSS TO PAY TITHES

PROVERBS 22:1

'If you have to choose between a good reputation and great wealth, choose a good reputation.'(GNB)

PHILIPPIANS 1:27

'Only let your manner of life be worthy of the gospel of Christ, so that whether I come and see you or am absent, I may hear of you that you are standing firm in one spirit, with one mind striving side by side for the faith of the gospel.'
(ESV)

Though the Bible admonishes Christians to pay tithes, be careful how you communicate this. It is easier when the congregation understands why they must pay tithes. Do not blackmail them to pay tithes. Do not use threatening language to coerce them to pay. Payment of tithes is an individual covenant between the believer and God. Your job ends at admonishing them gently to be obedient to God by fulfilling their financial obligations. An ill-informed congregation on tithing would create division in the church.

YOUNG PREACHER, YOU ARE DANGEROUS IF YOU CAN'T TALK ABOUT SIN

MATTHEW 3:1-2

'In those days John the Baptist came, preaching in the wilderness of Judea and saying, "Repent, for the kingdom of heaven has come near."'

(NASB)

Preaching about sin has become a very risky and dangerous venture in our churches these days. A pastor friend told me a couple of years ago that he has stopped preaching holiness and sin because he does not want to lose his members! This is very dangerous. God has given you this congregation to shepherd. It is your responsibility to keep them and present them holy and blameless to the Lord on the last day. If you refuse to preach about sin, and your congregation goes astray you have a lot to answer for. God will require the souls of all those who missed their salvation from your hand.

YOUNG PREACHER, NOT ALL OF US ARE MEANT TO BE IN FULL-TIME MINISTRY

MATTHEW 22:14

'For many are invited, but few are chosen.' (NIV)

Young minister, understand that not all ministers are meant to be in full-time ministry. The decision to go full time has wide-ranging consequences for your family and the church. If you are a professional, consider working and doing ministry part-time. This will help lift the financial burden off your family and the young church you are pastoring. When you get the understanding that ministry does not necessarily only happen from behind the pulpit, then irrespective of the work you do, you will lift the name of Christ there. If you are a teacher, your ministry will be to reach out to the students with the gospel and shape their lives. If you are in the health sector, it will be an opportunity to reach out to the sick and dying with the message of salvation and hope. It does not matter which profession you are involved in; you can always do ministry there. Do not jump into full-time ministry. Wait and listen to God first.

YOUNG PREACHER, ARE YOU SO PASSIONATE ABOUT THE PRAISE OF MEN?

JOHN 12:43
'For they loved human praise more than praise from God.' (NIV)

As a young preacher be careful of the praise of men. The Bible says that Jesus was not moved by the praise of men because He knew what was in the heart of men. Do not be too obsessed with the praise of men. It is a slippery slope that can lead to your downfall. As you do your ministry men will, by all means, show appreciation. Though this show of appreciation may be genuine, do not be taken in by it. It is God who has given you the opportunity to serve. His praise is what matters, and not what men tell you.

2
Young Itinerant Minister

CHAPTER TWO

Young Itinerant Minister

BE CONSCIOUS OF TIME

1 CORINTHIANS 14:32

'The spirits of prophets are subject to the control of prophets.' (NIV)

One of the ways you can gain credibility with your host pastor and his congregation is by sticking to your allocated time. Before you enter the auditorium, find out from your host what time you should be at the church auditorium and the time that has been allotted for you in the main programme. Once you have been given this information, do your best to be punctual. When you mount the pulpit to preach, stick to your allotted time. Desist from overshooting your time and blaming it on the anointing.

DON'T GO AS A BURDEN BUT AS A BLESSING

HEBREWS 3:2

'He was faithful to the one who appointed him, just as Moses was faithful in all God's house.'
(NIV)

When you are invited to preach at a church, go and be a blessing to your host. Do not become a burden to him. When going, take along gifts for your host's household.

Take along everything you will need for the duration you will be staying with them, or at the hotel. Please ensure you have necessities like sponge, brush, toothpaste and towel (if you are not staying in a hotel). Accept the hotel that you are booked into with gladness. Never make a fuss about the quality of the hotel. That may be the only hotel your host can afford. If it becomes necessary for you to make any adjustments (either change your hotel or upgrade your room) promptly inform your host about it, and discuss how any financial ramifications will be offset.

APPRECIATE ANY HONORARIUM YOU ARE GIVEN!

PHILIPPIANS 4:18

'I have received full payment and have more than enough. I am amply supplied, now that I have received from Epaphroditus the gifts you sent. They are a fragrant offering, an acceptable sacrifice, pleasing to God.' (NIV)

Do not murmur over the honorarium your host gives you. Be content with what you are given, and show appreciation. The truth is that most churches struggle to come up with the amount of money paid to you as honorarium. Some pastors go out of their way to top up your honorarium with their personal finances. Remember that you are not in ministry for the money. The honorarium is just a token to take care of some personal expenses you may have incurred as a result of your decision to attend the programme. In some instances, your host even takes care of your transportation costs, food and hotel accommodation. The honorarium in this instance only becomes a token of appreciation to you for your time. That is why you do not have any room to murmur!

DESIST FROM ALLOWING MEMBERS TO COME TO YOUR HOTEL ROOM FOR COUNSELLING

1 CORINTHIANS 10:13

'You are tempted in the same way that everyone else is tempted. But God can be trusted not to let you be tempted too much, and he will show you how to escape from your temptations.' (CEV)

When you minister in a church, it is very likely the church members would like to see you for counselling. You might even need to counsel some members if specific issues come up during your ministration. However, as far as it's practical, desist from encouraging such members from visiting your hotel room for counselling. Not only is it unethical, but it creates uncomfortable situations for your host pastor as well. If you must do counselling, do it in a recognised space, preferably in an office allocated to you by your host pastor, where the privacy of the session can be guaranteed. As a young minister, apply wisdom in these matters. Do not put yourself in a situation which will compromise your integrity, and further jeopardise your host pastor and yourself.

BE CONSIDERATE IN YOUR REQUESTS

PHILIPPIANS 4:5

'Let everyone see that you are considerate in all you do. Remember, the Lord is coming soon.' (NLT)

ROMANS 12:16

Live in harmony with each other. Don't be too proud to enjoy the company of ordinary people. And don't think you know it all! (NIV)

The truth is that a lot of churches are struggling financially. It is therefore prudent that when you accept to minister in a church you be measured in your demands. Do not make unreasonable demands of your host, and thereby put him under undue stress. Be modest. And be understanding if you do not get the luxury you have dreamt about.

DON'T GO TO IMPRESS

GALATIANS 6:12

'Those who want to impress people by means of the flesh are trying to compel you to be circumcised. The only reason they do this is to avoid being persecuted for the cross of Christ.' (NIV)

When you are invited to minister in any church, you are not there to impress anybody. The only reason you have been invited is to share the Word of God. The only person you should seek to impress is your Lord Jesus Christ whose servant you are. Avoid stepping into the trap of pleasing people. Doing that would sound the death knell for you. Choose your dresses, language, stagecraft and gesticulations carefully as the Spirit leads you, and not because you want to impress the congregation or your host. Do not forget that a lot of ministers killed their ministries because they sought to impress man.

DON'T CREATE A BAD IMAGE OF OTHER PASTORS SO YOU MONOPOLISE THAT PARTICULAR PULPIT

GALATIANS 5:15

'If you bite and devour each other, watch out or you will be destroyed by each other.' (NIV)

ISAIAH 33:1

'Woe to you, destroyer, you who have not been destroyed! Woe to you, betrayer, you who have not been betrayed! When you stop destroying, you will be destroyed; when you stop betraying, you will be betrayed.' (NIV)

As you minister, be careful not to create a bad image of other pastors just to make yourself look good. Yes, there might be some pastors who have strayed from their calling and may be engaged in ungodly behaviour. But do not use your host's pulpit to run them down, while projecting a positive image of yourself. As much as possible, stick to your message!

DO NOT CREATE CONFUSION AND DESTROY SOMEONE'S HARD WORK

EXODUS 22:5

'If anyone grazes their livestock in a field or vineyard and lets them stray and they graze in someone else's field, the offender must make restitution from the best of their own field or vineyard.' (NIV)

Recognise that your host may have laboured to build his congregation. It is not easy building up a congregation so when you get the opportunity to minister do not do anything that will scatter this congregation. Be mindful of your utterances. Be mindful of the alliances you keep. You may be unknowingly fuelling a division in the church. Just one bad word can create irreparable damage to the church and lead to a possible breakup. Be wise!

RESPECT YOUR HOST'S BELIEFS. IF YOU DISAGREE, TURN DOWN THE INVITATION

AMOS 3:3

'Do two walk together unless they have agreed to do so?' (NIV)

When you accept an invitation to minister at a church, it implies that your beliefs and those of your host align. As you minister, do not condemn your host's beliefs. Do not use your host's pulpit to launch an attack on their belief systems, no matter how awkward they may seem. If you feel strongly about these beliefs, do not accept the invitation in the first place. For instance, there is controversy in Christendom over whether women should cover their head when in church. Charismatic churches generally do not think it is necessary for women to cover their hair. Some conservative Pentecostals, however, observe strict adherence to the covering of hair by women. Irrespective of where you stand, do not go condemning your host if his/her position is at variance with yours.

ADD WISDOM TO YOUR PROPHETIC WORD!

1 CORINTHIANS 14:32

'The spirits of prophets are subject to the control of prophets.' (NIV)

A lot of homes and relationships are falling apart because of so-called prophecies. Some prophets give prophecies that tend to create fear and division instead of edifying members. Visiting Minister, God may have given you a Word. But in proclaiming this Word use wisdom. Certain prophecies should be communicated to the individual concerned privately. Do not make a public show of it just because you want everyone to know how powerful you are. Other prophecies should be communicated only to your host. Be careful not to leave a confused congregation behind after your programme.

DISCOURAGE MEMBERS FROM DISCUSSING YOUR HOST WITH YOU

ROMANS 14:4

'Who are you to judge someone else's servant? To their own master, servants stand or fall. And they will stand, for the Lord is able to make them stand.' (NIV)

Exercise extreme caution when relating to members of your host's congregation. Naturally, a few of them will gravitate towards you as a guest minister, and begin to badmouth their pastor to you. Do not entertain this practice. Never be a conduit through which members of the congregation vent their anger and frustration about their pastor. Consciously attempt to stay away from being drawn into any squabbles or conflicts in your host's church.

DESIST FROM STARTING A CHURCH CLOSE BY IN THE NAME OF 'GOD HAS SENT ME THERE'

ROMANS 15:20

'It has always been my ambition to preach the gospel where Christ was not known so that I would not be building on someone else's foundation.' (NIV)

It raises several ethical questions when the guest preacher who has been frequenting a particular church decides to establish a branch of his church in the same neighbourhood. Doing that will destroy the relationship you have with your host pastor. Similarly, do not under any circumstances pull away members of your host pastor's church in order to start your own church. This practice is demonic, and you will receive punishment for it.

ENSURE YOU HAVE CASH ON YOU FOR ANY EMERGENCIES

2 CORINTHIANS 4:8

'We are hard-pressed on every side, but not crushed; perplexed, but not in despair.' (NIV)

It is not such a good practice to request money from your host just because you do not have any money on you. Whenever you accept to minister in any church, go along with enough money on you. The money should be enough to take care of your needs while you are away. What you carry on you should be enough to take care of your accommodation, meals and transport, assuming your host does not provide these.

GUEST PASTOR, PLEASE GIVE AN OFFERING!

ACTS 20:35

'In everything I did, I showed you that by this kind of hard work we must help the weak, remembering the words the Lord Jesus himself said: "It is more blessed to give than to receive."'

(NIV)

During the offering time do not pretend to be in the spirit and let the offering basket pass. Giving offering is also part of your responsibilities. Like all other members of the congregation, give with joy and purity of heart. When you give your offering, you motivate other members of the church to also give their offering. Be an inspirer.

TRY TO BRING A GIFT TO YOUR HOST IF YOU CAN

ROMANS 12:13

'...contributing to the needs of the saints, practicing hospitality.' (NASB)

It is a tradition to get a gift for your host and his family. If possible, come along with a gift for your host family. Gift giving is a sign of goodwill. It also sends a clear message of friendship. Bringing a gift to your host also signals your readiness to work with him to advance the ministry work. This gift does not necessarily have to be anything extravagant or flamboyant. Think it through with your wife (if you are married) and select a gift that can best convey your intentions.

DON'T GO AND TRY TO PROVE TO THE MEMBERS THAT YOU ARE MORE POWERFUL THAN YOUR HOST

PROVERBS 27:2

'Let another praise you, and not your own mouth; a stranger, and not your own lips.' (ESV)

Beware of the danger of striving to prove to the church members that you are more powerful than your host. Maybe you operate in the more visible power gifts like healing and miracles. Do not project this gift above that of your host. The gift of the working of miracles is not in any way superior to the other gifts. Just be yourself, and ensure that at all times you show appreciation to your host for giving you his platform to preach from. Again, remember that your host has used years to build his church. Do not go and create any disaffection for him from his members.

ENSURE THAT YOUR OPENING REMARKS ACKNOWLEDGE ALL THE RELEVANT PEOPLE

ROMANS 13:7

'Give to everyone what you owe them: If you owe taxes, pay taxes; if revenue, then revenue; if respect, then respect; if honor, then honor.' (NIV)

Each time you are going to minister, ensure you acknowledge your host, his/her spouse, junior pastors, the leadership of the church, the church council as well as the entire church. It is a matter of courtesy to be grateful to them for opening their doors to you to come and do ministry. Showing gratitude will open further doors to you in the future.

WHAT WILL KEEP YOU RELEVANT IS YOUR INTEGRITY, NOT YOUR GIFT

PROVERBS 11:3

'The integrity of the upright guides them, but the unfaithful are destroyed by their duplicity.' (NIV)

You may be super-gifted. Maybe the Lord does signs and wonders through you. Maybe you prophesy. All of these are good. But what is more relevant is your integrity. Remember that the gift cannot be superior to the fruit. Bearing the fruit of the Spirit is what sets you apart as a child of God. It is not the gifts that you demonstrate. So please, check your attitude!

TREAT BOTH SMALL AND BIGGER CHURCHES THE SAME

TITUS 2:7

'In everything set them an example by doing what is good. In your teaching show integrity, seriousness...' (NIV)

Do not fall into the trap of being choosy over the churches whose invitations you accept to preach in based on congregation size. When an invitation comes to preach in a church, let the Holy Spirit have His way in deciding whether to accept the invitation or not. Do not be led by considerations like the financial status of the church, its popularity, influence, the clout of its senior pastor, etc. Be prayerful, and be sensitive to the Holy Spirit Who will make such decisions for you.

3

Young Minister

CHAPTER THREE

Young Minister

YOUNG MINISTER, DON'T BE MONEY-LED BUT SPIRIT-LED.

MATTHEW 6:24

'No one can serve two masters, for either he will hate the one and love the other, or he will be devoted to the one and despise the other. You cannot serve God and money.' (NIV)

We live in tough times, and as a young minister, finding your feet in ministry things can be much more financially difficult for you. However, no matter the level of your financial difficulty do not let money be the motivation for what you do in ministry. Always remember that when God calls you into ministry, He will also give you provisions to sustain you. Look up to Him. Let the Holy Spirit lead you in this journey that can sometimes be very rough.

ARROGANCE WILL ONLY BRING YOU DOWN.

PROVERBS 29:23

'Pride brings a person low, but the lowly in spirit gain honor.' (NIV)

A lot of promising young ministers have killed their ministries through arrogance. Be careful when God opens many doors for you, and you begin seeing success in ministry that you do not become haughty. Success in ministry can be a slippery slope. A number of ministers who were considered God's Generals went down at the height of their success. How does arrogance in ministry manifest? When you begin to demand heightened respect, and almost worship from your members, know that you are standing at the threshold of arrogance. When you begin to be selective about the kind of people you minister to, that is a sure sign that you are sliding into arrogance. When you demand to be addressed by titles, that is a sign of arrogance. Know that you serve at the pleasure of Jesus. You can therefore not take His place. Project Jesus and Him alone. Play second fiddle to Him.

DON'T FORCE PEOPLE TO BELIEVE WHAT YOU DO BELIEVE. YOUR JOB IS ONLY TO GOD.

EPHESIANS 2:8-9

'For by grace you have been saved through faith. And this is not your own doing; it is the gift of God, not a result of works, so that no one may boast.' (NIV)

There are diversities of gifts. So are there ministries. Your gift defines your ministry. You may be an evangelist. You do your ministry based on this calling. Someone else may be an apostle. He/she does ministry in accordance with this calling. Do not force people to accept your beliefs or way of doing things. Not everyone has the same calling as you. Your mandate is to fulfil your calling, not to compel people to believe what you believe.

NEVER THINK YOU HAVE THE KNOWLEDGE AND ANSWERS TO EVERY PROBLEM (NYANSA NNI BAAKOFO) TIRIMU)

PROVERBS 28:26

'He that trusteth in his own heart is a fool:
but whoso walketh wisely, he shall be delivered.'

(KJV)

It is a sign of spiritual arrogance for you to assume you know it all. You do not have the answers to all questions. Stop posturing that you are the "Mr All Knowledgeable". The reason God did not create you to be all-knowledgeable is for you to learn inter-dependence. When confronted with a question whose answer you do not have, fall on colleagues who have the answers you seek. Similarly, when you are preparing your sermon and you need to use illustrations from a field of study you are not familiar with, be humble enough to call up the experts to shed light on that topic for you. Do not go and embarrass yourself with your 'confident ignorance'. Do not underestimate your congregation.

SEEK REVELATION INTO THE WORD

ISAIAH 45:15

'Truly, You are a God who hides Himself,
O God of Israel, Savior!' (NASB)

Seek revelation into the Word of God. A minister must be a student of the Word. Spend a lot more time studying the Word of God to gain understanding and deep insight into events and things that happen in this world. As you stay connected to the Holy Spirit you gain a deeper knowledge of the Word. It is also necessary to speak to a mentor about things about ministry that you do not understand.

NEVER START A CHURCH WITH REBELS WHO FOLLOWED YOU TO BREAK AWAY

PROVERBS 3:30

'Do not accuse a man without cause, when he has done you no harm.' (BSB)

If you decide to break away from your parent church then go alone. Do not have a deliberate strategy to pull members of your old church away with you. Embark on a massive evangelism campaign to win souls. After you get the souls disciple them so that they remain in your new church. Do not destroy what someone has taken years to build.

MINISTRY IS NOT LED BY EMOTION

ROMANS 8:14

'For those who are led by the Spirit of God are the children of God.' (NIV)

As a minister of God, do not be led by your emotions. As you go about your duties let reason and sensitivity to the Holy Spirit lead you to make decisions. Do not be too emotional with people. For instance, there is no need for launching personal attacks on people you deem to be disruptive. Some ministers of God have caused irreparable damage to their ministries because they became too emotional over events that happened to them. Some got unnecessarily angry over some petty issues. Others got depressed because of betrayals. Whatever the circumstances it is important that you keep a handle on your emotions.

YOU SHOULD BE WILLING TO WALK ALONE SOMETIMES

GENESIS 32:24

'So Jacob was left alone, and a man wrestled with him till daybreak.' (NIV)

Ministry can sometimes be a lonely walk. Do not expect to have company at all times. There are moments of highs and lows. Develop the mental fortitude to be able to survive through such moments. After performing a most stunning miracle, by commanding fire from heaven to consume an altar soaked in water, Elijah entered into a depressive phase. He found himself alone. In the course of leading the children of Israel through the wilderness, Moses found himself alone at certain points. Listen carefully, young pastor: you can be surrounded by a crowd and still feel lonely. When you get to this point, remember that fellowship with God is the only option left.

DON'T JOIN OTHERS TO FIGHT

PROVERBS 24:21

'Fear the LORD and the king, my son, and do not join with rebellious officials.' (NIV)

Be careful you do not get drafted into an unnecessary fight. As a young minister, understand the political dynamics in the church. In some places, deacons and elders have issues with the pastor. Even within the church council itself, there might be divisions. At this point, if you are not careful, you might be lobbied to join one group or the other to fight against the other side. Watch out. Use wisdom, and avoid these internal conflicts. They impede the development of the church.

STOP TAKING THE PHONE NUMBERS OF OTHER PEOPLE'S CHURCH MEMBERS

EXODUS 22:1

'Whoever steals an ox or a sheep and slaughters it or sells it must pay back five head of cattle for the ox and four sheep for the sheep.' (NIV)

Whenever you visit any church, ensure you do not take the phone numbers of church members of your host, especially the key members. If for some reason you must take a number (maybe the person is a professional whose help you will need at a point in time), talk to your host about it. It is important not to develop a personal relationship with the members of your host church. This measure is necessary to avoid any ethical breaches.

SPEAKING EVIL ABOUT YOUR SENIOR PASTOR WILL CATCH UP WITH YOU ONE DAY

ROMANS 13:1-2

'Everyone must submit to governing authorities. For all authority comes from God, and those in positions of authority have been placed there by God. So anyone who rebels against authority is rebelling against what God has instituted, and they will be punished.' (NLT)

Check your relationship with your senior pastor. Develop a very positive relationship with him. He is the shepherd of your ministry life. There is so much he knows about ministry that you are only now learning. Be humble and learn. No handbook on ministry can be more helpful than the experience of your senior pastor. Tap into this experience. Treat him/her with the utmost respect. Do not be tempted to tell members of the congregation that you are better than he is. This move will be demonic. Remember, Lucifer fell because he felt he could be equal to God. Never badmouth your senior pastor. He is also a human being with human frailties common to all of us. Never use his weaknesses as an excuse to speak evil about him to members of the congregation. One day you may also be a senior pastor! Don't incite others because you want them to empathise with you and fight against your senior pastor.

BE CAREFUL NOT TO ENVY OTHERS

JAMES 3: 14-16
'But if you harbor bitter envy and selfish ambition in your hearts, do not boast about it or deny the truth. 15 Such "wisdom" does not come down from heaven but is earthly, unspiritual, demonic. 16 For where you have envy and selfish ambition, there you find disorder and every evil practice.' (NIV)

In life, there will always be someone who has more money than you. There will always be someone more handsome or beautiful than you. There will always be someone who receives more invitations to speak at international conferences than you. There will always be someone who married earlier than you and had their first child earlier than you. It is important you do not envy such people. Be content with what God has given you, and keep praying that He gives you the desires of your heart. If He called you into ministry, then He will fully equip you!

YOUNGER PASTOR, DO YOU READ YOUR BIBLE, DO YOU PRAY OR DO YOU RELY ON YOUR SKILL?

PROVERBS 3:5-6

'Trust in the Lord with all your heart, And lean not on your own understanding; In all your ways acknowledge Him, And He shall direct your paths.' (NKJV)

Success in ministry has nothing to do with any skill or theatrics. Young Pastor, success in ministry is not about your oratory skills, or how persuasively you can communicate. It is a combination of years of studying the Word, prayer and mentorship. Develop a personal Bible study plan for yourself, and spend time alone in prayer. Your strength comes from how long you spend communing with God. Let the Holy Spirit lead you, rather than relying on your skill.

LET'S LEARN TO TAKE A BREAK!

GENESIS 2: 2-3

'And on the seventh day God ended His work which He had done, and He rested on the seventh day from all His work which He had done.'
(NKJV)

Do not burn out in ministry. Work very hard. Give your all to your work but learn to take a break periodically. Taking a break does not mean that you are weak. No, it is a sign of strength. Jesus, after healing the sick and preaching to the multitudes, always retreated to a place by Himself. He also admonished His disciples to take a rest. You retreat to refresh yourself and refuel. It is also good for your health. So, Young Minister, learn to take a break. It could be a few days every month, or a week every quarter where you retreat to a secluded place and devote yourself to prayer and rest.

MINISTRY IS BUSY BUT FIND TIME FOR YOUR FAMILY, ESPECIALLY YOUR WIFE

1TIMOTHY 3:5

'If anyone does not know how to manage his own family, how can he take care of God's church?' (NIV)

1 TIMOTHY 5:8

'Anyone who does not provide for their relatives, and especially for their own household, has denied the faith and is worse than an unbeliever.'
(NIV)

While you do ministry, make sure that you find time for your family. God has not said anywhere that you should sacrifice your family for ministry. Your ministry work is easier when your family is well taken care of, especially psychologically and financially. Take a break and spend time with the family. You can take the entire family out somewhere and have some family time together for the weekend. Or you could take your kids to recreational centres each holiday or when they are on vacation. As you refresh them, they will also give you that spiritual and psychological support you need to succeed in ministry. If you neglect your wife, you will be miserable in ministry.

DO NOT FORCE YOUR WIFE TO DO MINISTRY LIKE YOU!

1 CORINTHIANS 7:7

'I wish that all men were as I am. But each man has his own gift from God; one has this gift, another has that.' (BSB)

You got a call to be in the ministry, not your wife. When you meet a woman who also has a calling and you choose to marry her, then that is a bonus for you. But do not under any circumstances force your wife to do ministry when she has not been called. Instead of intimidating her with your ministry call, why not encourage her to support you with whatever her calling is? If she is a teacher, how can she support your ministry? If she is a trader in the market, in what ways can she support your ministry? If she is a nurse, explore ways she can use her talent to support your ministry. It is suicidal to compel her to join you in mainstream ministry.

DON'T PREPARE FOR ONLY MINISTRY, PREPARE FOR MARRIAGE AS WELL.

RUTH 3:10-11

'And he said, Blessed be thou of the Lord, my daughter: for thou hast shewed more kindness in the latter end than at the beginning, inasmuch as thou followedst not young men, whether poor or rich. And now, my daughter, fear not; I will do to thee all that thou requirest: for all the city of

my people doth know that thou art a virtuous woman.' (KJV)

Young Minister, at some point you will probably get married. Prepare for marriage just as you would prepare for ministry work. Perhaps, besides your calling into ministry the other most important task you will have to undertake is work on your marriage. There is a direct relationship between the state of your marriage and success in ministry. If you have a happy and contented marriage, you will most likely have a successful ministry. So, as you busily prepare for ministry spend a lot of time preparing for your marriage as well.

YOUR FIRST MINISTRY IS YOUR FAMILY

1 TIMOTHY 3:5

'If anyone does not know how to manage his own family, how can he take care of God's church?' (NIV)

There is a principle you must understand as a young minister: your first ministry is your family. If you fail as a husband or wife, then you have already failed as a minister. That is why it is necessary to take very good care of your family first. Try your best to be a good father to your children, bringing them up in the fear of the Lord. Be a good husband to your wife. If you can support your family in the fear of the Lord then your ministry work becomes easier. Badly brought up children diminish your authority as a father to the congregation. You lose your moral authority to counsel couples in troubled marriages if you live in a troubled marriage yourself. So, fix your problems!

EXPLORE ALTERNATIVE SOURCES OF MAKING GENUINE INCOME

ACTS 20:34

'You yourselves know that these hands of mine have ministered to my own needs and those of my companions.' (NIV)

When you set out to do ministry, think of how you can make alternative sources of income so that you do not entirely rely on the church. It is becoming increasingly clear that church finances are dwindling, and, therefore, you cannot depend on the church for everything. You have to utilise the talent and knowledge that you have to earn extra income. For instance, if you are a professional teacher, you can take up a teaching appointment. If you are a health professional you could work part-time in a health facility. Or if you have business acumen you can start a small business or even go into consultancy. These avenues will give you some extra or additional income that you can use to support your family. It will also help ease financial pressures on you.

THINK ABOUT LIFE DURING PENSION

PROVERBS 6:6-11

'Go to the ant, you sluggard; consider its ways and be wise! It has no commander, no overseer or ruler, yet it stores its provisions in summer and gathers its food at harvest. How long will

you lie there, you sluggard? When will you get up from your sleep? A little sleep, a little slumber, a little folding of the hands to rest— and poverty will come on you like a thief and scarcity like an armed man.' (NIV)

You will inevitably retire at a certain point in your life if Christ tarries. Begin to make preparations for your pension right now. Find out if your church pays social security for its employees. There are also several other private pension schemes you can sign up to, making modest monthly contributions to support your retirement in future. Think not only of yourself but your family too, when you are no longer in active service.

DON'T LET TITLES GO TO YOUR HEAD

PROVERBS 23: 1:5

'When you sit down to eat with someone important, keep in mind who he is. If you have a big appetite, restrain yourself. Don't be greedy for the fine food he serves; he may be trying to trick you. Be wise enough not to wear yourself out trying to get rich. Your money can be gone in a flash, as if it had grown wings and flown away like an eagle.' (GNB)

Do not let the titles you have go to your head. It is not the titles you possess that define you or your ministry so stop being puffed up over some title you have. I witnessed an incident where one pastor got furious because the MC did not introduce him properly. According to him, the MC should have introduced him as 'Rev Dr' instead of the 'dry' title of 'Pastor'. Young Minister, you may have a doctorate degree or a master's degree. But these academic titles do not count. What matters is that you are a minister of the gospel of Jesus Christ, and your primary responsibility is towards the sheep in your care.

IF YOU CAN, HAVE JUST A FEW FRIENDS

PROVERBS 18:24

'A man of many companions may come to ruin, but there is a friend who sticks closer than a brother.' (ESV)

Friends play a transformational role in our lives. Depending on the type of friends you keep, your ministry can thrive or collapse. As much as possible, keep fewer friends, especially outside ministry circles. Some friends will only come into your life to disrupt your ministry. Others can also lead you astray. So, to avoid all these negative ramifications, keep as few friends as possible. If you must keep friends then they should be people who can inspire you to succeed in ministry.

4
Young Usher

CHAPTER FOUR

Young Usher

LEARN TO COME TO CHURCH ON TIME

1 CORINTHIANS 14:40

'But all things should be done decently and in order.' (ESV)

The first people who should arrive at church are the ushers. The auditorium needs to be ready for service each meeting day. Chairs have to be arranged. The altar has to be dusted. The floor has to be swept and kept clean. All these chores should be done very early. You, therefore, have no excuse to come to church late. When you are late, it affects every aspect of the service. Do not be the reason for holding up God at service!

MAKE MEMBERS AND GUESTS FEEL WELCOME

JAMES 2:1

'My brothers and sisters, practice your faith in our glorious Lord Jesus Christ by not favoring one person over another.' (NAS)

For example, two men come to your worship service. One man is wearing gold rings and fine clothes; the other man, who is poor, is wearing shabby clothes. Suppose you give special attention to the man wearing fine clothes and say to him, "Please have a seat." But you say to the poor man,

"Stand over there," or "Sit on the floor at my feet." Aren't you discriminating against people and using a corrupt standard to make judgments?' (NAS)

When a first-timer enters the church auditorium, the feeling they get should compel them to keep coming to worship with you. That can only be possible when they get a 'royal' treat from the ushers. Dear Usher, please help the guests who come to your church feel welcome. Speak politely to them. Give them a warm smile and be courteous to them, even when they are rude.

BE EXTRAVAGANT WITH YOUR SMILE.

1 PETER 4: 8-9

'Above all, love each other deeply, because love covers over a multitude of sins. Offer hospitality to one another without grumbling.' (NIV)

LEVITICUS 19: 33-34

'When a foreigner resides among you in your land, do not mistreat them. The foreigner residing among you must be treated as your native-born. Love them as yourself, for you were foreigners in Egypt. I am the LORD your God.' (NIV)

If you naturally struggle to smile, then you may have to work on it. Learn how to smile and be pleasant to people. This is because when guests are entering the church they need to be met with a warm smile. It helps them to feel at ease. Let them feel welcome by your smile. A smile will make a whole world of difference to somebody. You might not know the number of lives you would have saved by smiling. As an usher, your smile is your most potent tool. Deploy it generously.

STOP DISCRIMINATING: IF IT'S A HANDSHAKE, IT'S A HANDSHAKE FOR ALL, NOT SOME

ACTS 10:34

'So Peter opened his mouth and said: "Truly I understand that God shows no partiality."'(ESV)

As an usher, you mustn't be seen to be discriminating on any basis. There is always a perception that ushers are favourably predisposed to relaxing the rules for richer and more well-connected members of the congregation. This perception has to be broken. If you are required to give a handshake, go ahead and give one to everyone who walks into the auditorium. Do not look at a person's manner of dress or disposition and refuse them a handshake. If your friend walks through the door, treat them like any other person. It is not the time to be chatty and exceptionally congenial. This is necessary so that you do not give the impression that you discriminate in your attitude towards guests.

YOUR DUTIES PROHIBIT YOU FROM BEING AT LOGGERHEADS WITH ANYONE IN CHURCH

ROMANS 12:18

'If it is possible, as far as it depends on you, live at peace with everyone.' (NIV)

Do everything possible to avoid creating bad blood between yourself and anyone in the church. In the course of performing your duties, you will encounter all kinds of characters, some of whom may step on your toes. Some may provoke you. Others may deliberately stretch your patience to elastic limits. In all these circumstances, maintain a high level of emotional intelligence by not reacting in proportion to the level of provocation. Just be professional and do your job. Do not take things personally. Relate well with everyone in church.

CHOOSE YOUR WORDS CAREFULLY. YOU'RE SOMEONE'S SERMON!

PHILIPPIANS 1:27

'Whatever happens, conduct yourselves in a manner worthy of the gospel of Christ. Then, whether I come and see you or only hear about you in my absence, I will know that you stand firm in the one Spirit, striving together as one for the faith of the gospel.' (NIV)

As an usher, you are the face of the church. You are the first point of contact for the guest visiting your church for the first time. For some of these guests, you are the best sermon they will hear, not the one the pastor preaches. So please, put on your best smile. Some people enter the church with hurt in their hearts. Some run to church because they have been wounded and want a place to get respite. Do not compound their problems. By encountering you, may they receive the healing they desperately require.

YOUNG USHER, STOP GOSSIPING ABOUT PEOPLE'S DRESSES AND OUTFITS

EXODUS 23:1

'Do not spread false reports. Do not help a guilty person by being a malicious witness.' (NIV)

LEVITICUS 19:16

'Do not go about spreading slander among your people. Do not do anything that endangers your neighbor's life. I am the LORD.' (NIV)

You are the first point of contact for members of the congregation and guests alike. This privilege does not mean that you can turn people's way of dressing into a subject for gossip. It is unacceptable for groups of ushers to huddle in a corner and gossip about people's dressing for church. If you do this, you will only bring division to the church. When you gossip, you also drive people away from the church. If you make fun of someone who wears tattered clothes to church, you can be sure that they will not come to church again. Remember, if they lose their salvation as a result you will answer for it.

DECENT DRESSING IS KEY

1 TIMOTHY 2:9-10

'Likewise also that women should adorn themselves in respectable apparel, with modesty and self-control, not with braided hair and gold or pearls or costly attire, but with what is proper for women who profess godliness—with good works.' (ESV)

As an usher, please dress decently. Be a good representation of the church. Let people see the values the church cherishes through you. Let your dressing be a witness for Christ. To avoid issues of indecent dressing the ushering department should use uniforms. All ushers should wear uniforms that are decent, attractive and stylish.

YOUR ASSIGNMENT IS DANGEROUS. BE PRAYERFUL!

1 THESSALONIANS 5: 16-18

'Rejoice always, pray without ceasing, give thanks in all circumstances; for this is the will of God in Christ Jesus for you.' (ESV)

As an usher, your work exposes you to all kinds of danger, both spiritual and physical. You are usually the first person the guest encounters. You shake hands with them. Through this process, you could be exposed to some spiritual attacks. Physically, you could also be exposed to all manner of communicable diseases. This requires that you become prayerful. Be constantly praying and soaking yourself in the blood of Jesus. Before you go on duty each day make sure you spend quality time praying and securing your life and that of your colleagues with the blood of Jesus. Being slack in prayer means you are setting yourself up for danger.

DON'T BE TEMPTED TO STEAL CHURCH MONEY

1 TIMOTHY 6:10

'For the love of money is a root of all kinds of evil. Some people, eager for money, have

wandered from the faith and pierced themselves with many griefs.' (NIV)

If you are privileged to be part of the ushers who collect and count money, show the highest level of integrity. Do not see it as an opportunity to be stealing money. Remember, the money you collect and count represent people's prayers and covenants with God. If you touch it, you are inviting curses on yourself. Avoid the temptation of stealing church money, no matter how financially hard up you are.

KNOW THE NUMBER OF PEOPLE A GUEST PREACHER IS BRINGING AND PREPARE!

PROVERBS 24:27

'Prepare your work outside; get everything ready for yourself in the field, and after that build your house.' (ESV)

Head Usher (or Chief Usher, as some choose to call it), liaise with the protocol department and get information on the number of people a guest preacher is bringing so that you can make provision for them in terms of seating arrangements. Do this ahead of time. Similarly, when there is an event that members of the public will be attending, speak to the organisers and get a handle on the number of people to expect. This will help you decide if you need additional seats. Furthermore, get to know the dignitaries who will be coming so that you prepare their seats accordingly.

AGAIN, LET YOUR WORDS BE SEASONED

COLOSSIANS 4:6

'Let your speech be always with grace, seasoned with salt, that ye may know how ye ought to answer every man.' (KJV)

The work of ushering can sometimes be frustrating. You encounter all kinds of characters, some of them very saucy. Some guests can also be very difficult to deal with. They will refuse the seat offered them. In all these circumstances maintain calm as an usher. Never let any filthy words escape your mouth in reaction to what a guest does or says. Be professional in your work in the House of God!

USHERS DON'T LIKE TAKING NOTES DURING SERMONS. REPENT!

HABAKKUK 2:2

'Then the LORD replied: "Write down the revelation and make it plain on tablets so that a herald may run with it."' (NIV)

Do not pretend to be too busy that you miss the time for preaching. You also need nourishment from the Word of God. When it is time for the preaching, sit comfortably somewhere, pay attention and take notes as well. You cannot be too busy that you miss the Word of God.

MALE USHERS, STOP TAKING LADIES' PHONE NUMBERS AT THE ENTRANCE

JAMES 4: 4-6

'You're cheating on God. If all you want is your own way, flirting with the world every chance you get, you end up enemies of God and his way. And do you suppose God doesn't care? The proverb has it that "he's a fiercely jealous lover." And what he gives in love is far better than anything else you'll find.' (MSG)

Male ushers, it is unethical to take numbers of female guests to the church at the entrance. Focus on your task of ushering guests into the auditorium and making them feel comfortable. Do not take advantage of your task to forge 'unholy' alliances. If you genuinely want to build a relationship then do so outside church time. While on duty put on your best professional side.

5

Young First Lady,
Asafo Maame,
Pastor's Wife

CHAPTER FIVE

Young First Lady, Asafo Maame, Pastor's Wife

DON'T USE THE CHURCH AGAINST YOUR HUSBAND

EPHESIANS 5:22-24

'Wives, submit yourselves unto your own husbands, as unto the Lord. For the husband is the head of the wife, even as Christ is the head of the church: and he is the saviour of the body. Therefore as the church is subject unto Christ, so let the wives be to their own husbands in everything.' (KJV)

Do not at any point in time incite the church against your husband. The church is your husband's sacred platform. He earns deep respect from the church. It will be devastating to turn the church against him. Stop speaking ill about your husband to members of the church. Stop undermining the authority of your husband the pastor. When you do, eventually you will succeed in ruining your husband's ministry. When the pastor gives a directive that you do not agree with, or which in your view will lead to some negative consequences, speak to him at home to rectify it. Never make yourself the 'good guy' by fighting these directives in public. You will only end up undermining him and ultimately destroying him. When this happens, that will also have dire consequences for you and your children.

DON'T BRING ENMITY BETWEEN HIM AND THE MEMBERS BECAUSE YOU WANT ATTENTION

TITUS 2:4-5

'Then they can urge the younger women to love their husbands and children, to be self-controlled and pure, to be busy at home, to be kind, and to be subject to their husbands, so that no one will malign the word of God.' (NIV)

Generally, women want attention. This has been established by relevant literature. The nature of ministry work is such that the pastor interacts with a number of church members, who are mostly females. Understand your husband's ministry, and stop being jealous when others demand some attention from him. Right from the beginning of your marriage understand that the nature of your husband's work means that you will literally be sharing his attention with members of the congregation. All he needs from you is your understanding.

STOP SKIPPING CHURCH BECAUSE YOU AND THE PASTOR (YOUR HUSBAND) ARE QUARRELLING

PHILIPPIANS 2:12

'Wherefore, my beloved, as ye have always obeyed, not as in my presence only, but now

much more in my absence, work out your own
salvation with fear and trembling.' (KJV)

Do not use going to church as a bargaining chip whenever you quarrel with your husband. As a Christian, you also need nourishment from the Word of God, and also to fellowship with other believers. You do not go to church because of your husband. Whatever wrong your husband has committed against you personally cannot be a reason for you to stop going to church. You are a Christian first, before a First Lady.

PRAY FOR HIM

COLOSSIANS 2:7

'...rooted and built up in him, strengthened in the
faith as you were taught, and overflowing with
thankfulness.' (NIV)

The best support you can give to your husband is consistent prayer. Understand that your husband's ministry is a spiritual one, and he is at the forefront of vicious spiritual battles. Some of the enemies may come from the church. Sometimes the pastor may be so consumed with doing church work that he might find very little time to pray. As a wife, you are his pillar. When he is so tired that he falls asleep during prayer time, cover him with your prayers. Be diligent in prayer. Declare some days of fast, even without his knowledge, and intercede for him and the ministry he does. Never forget that a prayer-less wife becomes a conduit for spiritual attacks on the husband.

DON'T USE YOUR EMOTIONS AND POSITION TO INFLUENCE THE CHURCH BOARD'S DECISIONS

ROMANS 12:2

'Do not be conformed to this world, but be transformed by the renewal of your mind, that by testing you may discern what is the will of God, what is good and acceptable and perfect.' (ESV)

Your husband works with a church council or board. This body is responsible for taking major decisions on behalf of the church. The pastor is bound by the decisions of the board or council. Sometimes these decisions may not be palatable to you as a person. When that happens, do not seek to influence this decision in any way. You are a powerful mother of the church. But do your best to draw a line between your domestic duties as a wife, and the administrative decisions of the church. Do not abuse your role as the wife of the pastor by interfering in decisions of the church council or board.

DON'T RUSH FOR PULPITS

PROVERBS 21:3

'To do righteousness and justice is more acceptable to the Lord than sacrifice.' (ESV)

1 SAMUEL 15:22

'And Samuel said, "Has the Lord as great delight in burnt offerings and sacrifices, as in obeying the voice of the Lord? Behold, to obey is better than sacrifice, and to listen than the fat of rams."' (ESV)

Some First Ladies have their own ministry calling. But so long as you have not started your own church, and still worship with your husband in the same congregation, be very cautious of any self-projection tendencies. Do not rush for the pulpit. Do not do anything to overshadow your husband's ministry. Stand at the pulpit only when you are asked to do so. Subject yourself to the direction of your husband and the church council. Do not think because of your privileged position that you are free to take the pulpit anytime you wish. It will be tantamount to offering unholy fire before the Lord. God respects order. And so must you.

LET YOUR MAIN PRIORITY BE TO BRING UP YOUR CHILDREN WELL

PROVERBS 22:6
'Train up a child in the way he should go, And when he is old he will not depart from it.' (NKJV)

The good upbringing of your children should occupy your attention. People are going to judge your performance as a wife by how well you are able to bring up your children in the Christian faith. As someone who spends more time with the children (since the pastor may be busy doing ministry), you have a much bigger responsibility to ensure the children learn about the basic tenets of Christianity from you. Do not give room for people to blame your children's waywardness on you. When your husband travels, ensure that you lead the children in devotion. Ensure that they study their Bibles, and spend quiet time. If you notice they are struggling with it then you can do it together with them, and let it be fun-filled. When you hear any negative reports from people outside your home or church regarding how any of your children have behaved, take time to investigate, and when you have established the truth, mete out the necessary punishment. This will serve notice to the kids that you uphold sound Biblical standards.

NEVER HAVE PREFERENCES AMONG THE CHURCH MEMBERS

JAMES 2:1-4

'My brothers and sisters, you are believers in our glorious Lord Jesus Christ. So treat everyone the same. Suppose a man comes into your meeting wearing a gold ring and fine clothes. And suppose a poor man in dirty old clothes also comes in. Would you show special attention to the man wearing fine clothes? Would you say, "Here's a good seat for you"? Would you say to the poor man, "You stand there"? Or "Sit on the floor by my feet"? If you would, aren't you treating some people better than others? Aren't you like judges who have evil thoughts?' (NIRV)

As the First Lady of the church, you are considered a mother to every church member. Due to this heavy responsibility that's thrust on you be careful you are not seen to be having preferences among church members. It is natural that you will gravitate towards a few members who are committed and share the same ideals with you but do not despise the others. Draw everyone to yourself. Whatever you do for one, do for everyone. When giving gifts, give to all without showing any preference for any person or groups of persons. You must also be careful you are not drawn into any unofficial groupings in the church.

NEVER BE AT LOGGERHEADS WITH A CHURCH MEMBER

PSALM 37:8

'Refrain from anger, and forsake wrath!
Fret not yourself; it tends only to evil.' (ESV)

The responsibilities of being First Lady, especially of a large congregation, can be very daunting. You are dealing with very complex and complicated issues in church. In the midst of all these, you are expected to maintain your cool. In dealing with all kinds of characters, it is possible to have a run-in with some members of the church. Please, let it go. Do not be at loggerheads with any church member. You are revered as the Mother of the Church. So please, have a large heart. Some church members will deliberately create issues where there are none. Handle such cases with wisdom. Never be drawn into any conflicts. It will undermine your authority as a mother.

BE PREPARED, SOME MEMBERS WILL ALWAYS SEEK FOR YOUR HUSBAND'S ATTENTION

MATTHEW 6: 34

'Give your entire attention to what God is doing
right now, and don't get worked up about what

*may or may not happen tomorrow. God will help
you deal with whatever hard things come up
when the time comes.'* (MSG)

Deciding to marry a pastor comes with its own 'cross'. Your husband is also the 'husband' to many women in the church. He is a 'father' to the entire church. Due to these roles, everyone will be seeking his attention. Exercise patience and understand when this happens. When families face a crisis, the first person that comes to mind is your husband. Pastor will receive calls at odd times in the night. He will be called to visit the sick at the hospital on an emergency. Sometimes he may have to travel unannounced. Other times you will have to give out the little money you have saved for your family. Entertain strangers in your home on behalf of your husband. Members of the congregation will crowd your space. That is the cross you have to bear. Bear it with dignity!

BE A GATHERER; DON'T SCATTER

MATTHEW 12:30
*'Whoever is not with me is against me, and
whoever does not gather with me scatters.'* (NIV)

Being First Lady of the church means you are your husband's number one cheerleader. Help him build his ministry. Support him as he gathers. Do not scatter. This is important to him because ministry work is usually very stressful. In most cases, you are the only one who can offer a ray of hope to the pastor. It will be disastrous for you to scatter what he has taken years to build. Sometimes it might not be a conscious attempt at scattering but for instance, a simple act of smiling and being kind can help 'gather'. On the other hand, a quarrelsome wife will no doubt contribute to scattering her husband's hard work.

6
Church Member

CHAPTER SIX

Church Member

WHEN FAMILIARITY SETS IN, IT COULD IMPEDE YOUR GROWTH

PROVERBS 25:17

'Withdraw thy foot from thy neighbour's house; lest he be weary of thee, and so hate thee.' (KJV)

Your pastor or church leaders may be down to earth, and very approachable. As a result, you may have direct access to them. Consider this a privilege. Do not abuse it. Do not let familiarity set in, to the point where you treat them with disrespect. Never forget that your pastor is the shepherd over your soul. After everything is said and done, he stands in the gap between you and God. Honour him. Respect him. Do not let familiarity be the reason you will not be receiving any blessings from him.

DON'T COMPARE YOUR PASTOR TO THE GUEST PREACHER. THEIR ASSIGNMENTS ARE DIFFERENT

GALATIANS 6:4-6

'Don't compare yourself with others. Just look at your own work to see if you have done anything to be proud of. You must each accept the responsibilities that are yours.' (ERV)

Never, ever compare your pastor to a guest preacher who visits your church. Maybe you were impressed with the style of the preaching of that pastor who visited you. Maybe you love the fact that they prophesied and did a lot of fanciful things. Remember, they are guest preachers. Their assignment is only for a short period. When they finish their assignment and they leave, it is your pastor who will nurse and nurture you with the Word of God and ensure you grow in your faith. If the guest preacher said or did something wrong it is your pastor who will have to correct it.

CHURCH MEMBER, YOUR PASTOR IS NOT SUPER-HUMAN

COLOSSIANS 3:13-23

'Make allowance for each other's faults, and forgive anyone who offends you. Remember, the Lord forgave you, so you must forgive others. Above all, clothe yourselves with love, which binds us all together in perfect harmony.' (NLT)

He may be a pastor, but he is human. Be measured in your expectations of your pastor. He needs prayers, just as you also need prayers. He gets tired, just as you also do. He also has emotions just as you do. Sometimes when he is provoked, he can also get angry. Other times he is very happy. He may not physically show anger or hurt. But when he is betrayed, he feels hurt too. So, your pastor needs your understanding and support, rather than your condemnation.

REMEMBER SOME PASTORS ARE LEADING BUT BLEEDING. KEEP YOUR PASTOR IN YOUR PRAYERS

MATTHEW 16:24-26

'Then Jesus told his disciples, "If anyone would come after me, let him deny himself and take up his cross and follow me. For whoever would save his life will lose it, but whoever loses his life for my sake will find it. For what will it profit a man if he gains the whole world and forfeits his soul? Or what shall a man give in return for his soul?' (ESV)

Physically, your pastor may be wearing a beautiful smile. But inwardly he may be bleeding. Pastors go through a lot. It is not easy shepherding God's people. Imagine one pastor carrying the burdens of a congregation of one hundred and over! It is not easy. They only keep going because of the extraordinary grace of God upon their lives. The last thing they need from you is nagging, murmuring and backbiting. As a committed church member, support your pastor by devoting some time every day in intercession for him. Call to check on him once in a while. You have no idea what this does for him. Let your pastor feel loved and appreciated. If touched, you can also bless him with material things. Let us all help to support our pastors to enable them to have the peace of mind to execute God's assignment for them.

CHURCH MEMBER, FOCUS ON THE POSITIVES OF THE CHURCH, NOT ONLY ON THE NEGATIVES

EPHESIANS 4:2-3

'...with all humility and gentleness, with patience, bearing with one another in love, eager to maintain the unity of the Spirit in the bond of peace.' (ESV)

Church member, be more loyal and committed to the church. Stop badmouthing the church to outsiders. Every church has its issues. The church is the bride of Christ. Till we are raptured to be with the Lord we shall continue on this earth, with all our shortcomings and frailties. This, however, does not mean that you should keep hyping on the negatives of the church. There are many positive things you can discuss with outsiders about your church. You can talk about your church's passion for souls. You can talk about the great sermons that are delivered each Sunday. You can even talk about the wonderful brotherliness that exists among the congregants. These are things that can even draw people to the church. Be loyal to your church!

CHURCH MEMBER, WHY DO YOU RESPECT WORK TIME BUT NOT CHURCH TIME?

ACTS 9:31

'So the church throughout all Judea and Galilee and Samaria enjoyed peace, being built up; and going on in the fear of the Lord and in the comfort of the Holy Spirit, it continued to increase.' (NASB)

Is it not ironic that you will never go to work late? Or get to the airport late when travelling? But you feel no sense of shame or remorse going to church late! It is not all right to go to church late. Change your habit. It is the highest form of disrespect to God when you go to church late. No excuse can assuage the negative ramifications of this despicable habit. If you are scared of offending your boss (and therefore losing your salary), and so you go to work on time, you should be more worried about the eternal consequences of missing an appointment with God.

CHURCH MEMBER, IF YOU WANT GROWTH, STAY WHERE YOU ARE PLANTED!

1 CORINTHIANS 16:13

'Be on the alert, stand firm in the faith, act like men, be strong.' (NASB)

The English have a saying that 'a rolling stone gathers no moss'. You will never experience growth as a Christian if you hop from one church to the other. Swallow your pride, and stop getting offended with any pastor who rebukes you. Stay under the feet of one pastor, and learn from him. As you keep learning, you grow. As you go through different experiences (both positive and negative) in your church you will keep growing. God had a purpose for planting you where you are now.

CHURCH MEMBER, HAVE SOCIAL LIFE ASIDE CHURCH. IT'S GOOD FOR THE MIND

LUKE 5:29

'And Levi gave a big reception for Him in his house; and there was a great crowd of tax collectors and other people who were reclining at the table with them.' (NASB)

It is good that you have given your whole life to the church. But as a human being learn to have a social life. Find time to fraternise with people outside church. There are many godly social activities you can engage in. You can start a youth club in your neighbourhood committed to sharing the gospel. You can also join a musical or drama group in your neighbourhood. Once in a while take some time off and go on a holiday. Visit places like museums, pleasure gardens, amusement parks, etc. Churches must also leave room in the church calendar for socialising. There is a need for holistic development of church members.

FIND SOMETHING TO DO IN CHURCH

2 TIMOTHY 2:20

'In a large house there are articles not only of gold and silver, but also of wood and clay; some are for special purposes and some for common use.' (NIV)

Do not just be running around the church. find a department or ministry that appeals to you and join. Be an active member of the church, not just an anonymous churchgoer.

Carefully assess your spiritual gifts, your personality traits or temperament and then select a suitable department or ministry based on that. There are many advantages in joining a group in church. It is a proven fact that church members who join a group in church also tend to live righteous lives. You will also be using your spiritual gifts if you joined a group today. Refusal to join a group is similar to the servant who dug the ground and hid his master's talent. In the Scriptures, he was punished severely for not using the talent his master gave him. So, think twice!

PAY WELFARE DUES SO THAT YOU CAN BENEFIT FROM THE WELFARE SYSTEM IN TIMES OF NEED

2 CORINTHIANS 9:7

'Each one must give as he has decided in his heart, not reluctantly or under compulsion, for God loves a cheerful giver.' (ESV)

One of your responsibilities as a church member is to contribute to welfare dues. The welfare funds are usually used to support members who go through bereavement, or have weddings or are sick. It is a symbolic gesture to prove that the church, apart from its divine mandate, also takes the personal lives of its members seriously. Due to its significance, most churches encourage members to make periodic contributions to the welfare fund. Unfortunately, some members deliberately refuse to contribute anything to the fund. Ironically, they are the ones who seriously expect to receive support in moments of difficulty. Church member, understand that if you do not contribute anything to welfare, then do not expect any support from welfare.

YOU ARE A HYPOCRITE IF YOU WORSHIP YOUR PASTOR BUT DISRESPECTS YOUR HUSBAND!

EPHESIANS 5:33

'However, let each one of you love his wife as himself, and let the wife see that she respects her husband.' (ESV)

A sickening trend in Christianity these days is emerging, where women members of the church show gross disrespect to their husbands at home but virtually worship their pastors. This is demonic. Your husband is your head, not the pastor. If anybody deserves reverence from you, it should be your husband. Stop this hypocrisy of pretending to lie down for your pastor to walk on you but when you go home you treat your husband like rubbish. Cherish your husbands. Let everybody know how much you value them. Show respect to them both privately and publicly.

STOP THREATENING YOUR PASTOR THAT YOU WILL STOP COMING TO CHURCH

1 TIMOTHY 5:17-18

'Give double honor to spiritual leaders who handle their duties well. This is especially true if they work hard at teaching God's word. After all, Scripture says, "Never muzzle an ox when it is threshing grain," and "The worker deserves his pay."' (GWT)

Stop threatening your pastor that you will leave church. The church does not belong to your pastor. It belongs to God. You are jeopardising your salvation if you decide to leave church because of a personal issue you have with the pastor. Your pastor is a human being like you. He has his weaknesses just like you. If for some reason you have your problem with the pastor, then deal with it. Leave the church out of it. It will be regrettable to lose your salvation because you decided to elevate these personal issues.

WHY SHOULD THE CHURCH SUFFER BECAUSE OF YOUR ISSUES WITH SOMEONE IN THE CHURCH?

2 TIMOTHY 2:14

'Keep reminding God's people of these things. Warn them before God against quarreling about words; it is of no value, and only ruins those who listen.' (NIV)

Some people who have issues with some individual members of the church tend to vent their anger on the church. They can go to the extent of maligning the church and everything it stands for. They also badmouth the leadership of the church for some perceived actions or inactions. This attitude is not healthy. When you have personal issues with another member of the church it is best to resolve It amicably, preferably with the church leadership or some elders of the church. Do not rope in the church. That individual is not the church. And while you are busily smearing the image of the church because of your personal troubles you would do well to examine your role in the crisis. Maybe if you had behaved differently the crisis would have been averted.

IF YOU CANNOT SUBMIT THEN LEAVE AND GO TO WHERE YOU DON'T HAVE TO BUT YOU WON'T FIND ANYWHERE!

1 PETER 2:13-17

'Submit yourselves for the Lord's sake to every human authority: whether to the emperor, as the supreme authority, or to governors, who are sent by him to punish those who do wrong and to commend those who do right. For it is God's will that by doing good you should silence the ignorant talk of foolish people. Live as free people, but do not use your freedom as a cover-up for evil; live as God's slaves. Show proper respect to everyone, love the family of believers, fear God, honor the emperor.' (NIV)

You cannot be a part of a church where you find it difficult to submit to the leadership. Every Christian has a responsibility to respect authority. This includes both church and secular authority. At any point in time if you feel you cannot submit to your church leadership then it is probably time to leave. As you make up your mind to leave, you must remember one thing: wherever you go there will be an authority you must submit to.

STOP COMING TO CHURCH LATE AND YET YOU COMPLAIN THAT CHURCH CLOSES LATE!

GALATIANS 6:1

'Brothers, if anyone is caught in any transgression, you who are spiritual should restore him in a spirit of gentleness. Keep watch on yourself, lest you too be tempted.' (ESV)

In the church I attend, we start service at 8 am and close at 10:30 am. There is this particular lady who always comes to church at 10 am without fail. As soon as she sits down, she looks at her watch and starts fidgeting with her purse. She's eager to leave as quickly as possible. As soon as we close, she will be the first to leave. Why are people like that? Coming to church on time is a divine responsibility we have to carry out.

WHY DOES PRAYER SERVICE REGISTER LOWER ATTENDANCE?

EPHESIANS 4:15

'...but speaking the truth in love, we are to grow up in all aspects into Him who is the head, even Christ.' (NASB)

It is amazing that church prayer meetings register the lowest attendance. It is becoming increasingly clear that contemporary Christians do not like to pray. Even though the Bible tells to pray without ceasing, and not to forsake the assembly of the saints, we hardly respond positively when there is a prayer meeting. This is in sharp contrast to prophetic meetings. Or wealth creation seminars where you have full auditoriums. Our priorities as Christians have changed. No wonder most Christians are struggling spiritually in life.

STOP GOSSIPING ABOUT YOUR PASTOR AND YET YOU 'PAPA' HIM

PROVERBS 29:12

'When a leader listens to malicious gossip, all the workers get infected with evil.' (MSG)

Those of you who love to gossip about your pastor, and yet when you see him you pretend to love him, repent. It is sheer hypocrisy. Those of you who spend a considerable amount of your time gossiping about your pastor, repent! Why should you gossip about your pastor's dress sense? Why should you gossip about something the pastor has supposedly done? Why should you gossip about the pastor's family? You do all these to your pastor, and yet when you meet him you sweet-talk him as if you love him. Some of these same people will give testimonies and pour accolades on the pastor. God has seen what is in your heart. Repent!

THEY ARE DANGEROUS IF THEY STRUGGLE TO PROVE THEY ARE BETTER THAN YOUR PASTOR!

MATTHEW 7:12

'So whatever you wish that others would do to you, do also to them, for this is the Law and the Prophets.' (ESV)

In every church, there are those leaders and members who have constituted themselves into a 'Sanhedrin'. All they do is to criticise everything the pastor does and therefore try to prove to everyone that they are better than he is. At all times they scheme to make ministry difficult for the pastor. Sometimes they do it openly, but in most cases, they do it subtly. Stay away from such people. They can be destructive. They are like snake venom – very poisonous. Whenever a new member is identified as promising they get close to such a person and serve him/her their cup of poison against the pastor.

STOP GIVING GIFTS TO GUEST MINISTERS IF YOU ARE NOT GENEROUS TO YOUR PASTOR

GALATIANS 6:9

'And let us not be weary in well doing: for in due season we shall reap, if we faint not.' (KJV)

When was the last time you gave your pastor a gift? You have never given him any gift, not even on Pastor's Appreciation Day, his birthday or even on Christmas. Yet you give gifts to each guest minister who visits your church. Your pastor is the shepherd of your soul. When you have issues, it is your pastor you will run to. So, cherish your pastor. Yes, it is good to show generosity to guest ministers who visit your church. But do not do for them what you do not do for your pastor.

STOP COLLECTING CHANGE AFTER EVERY OFFERING

It is bizarre to collect change after every offering. Before you leave the house for church, try to get the right amount of change for offering purposes if you have higher denominations which you do not want to place in the offering bowl or basket. It is embarrassing to chase ushers to give you change for the offering you gave.

WHEN WAS THE LAST TIME YOU PRAYED FOR YOUR PASTOR?

1 TIMOTHY 2:1-2

'First of all, then, I urge that supplications, prayers, intercessions, and thanksgivings be made for all people, for kings and all who are in high positions, that we may lead a peaceful and quiet life, godly and dignified in every way.' (ESV)

When last did you pray for your pastor? Church members are quick to take their pastor to the cleaners for the slightest mistake he commits. But they hardly ever pray for him. Your pastor is also human. He also comes under attacks. Imagine one person carrying the spiritual burden of the entire church. It takes grace. That is why you must be constantly praying for your pastor. Devote time and pray for him. If possible, devote one day in the week to fast and pray for your pastor. Commit him into God's hands that he will remain steadfast and committed to his work in the Lord's vineyard. You shouldn't only pray for the pastor. Pray also for his family that God should use them as instruments to promote His work, and not as tools in the hands of the devil. Pray that your pastor will escape the fate of High Priest Eli who lost God's favour because of his children's disobedience.

STOP GOSSIPING ABOUT THE ASAFO MAAME (FIRST LADY)

ECCLESIASTES 10:20

'Don't bad-mouth your leaders, not even under your breath, And don't abuse your betters, even in

*the privacy of your home. Loose talk has a way
of getting picked up and spread around. Little
birds drop the crumbs of your gossip far and
wide.'* **(MSG)**

The First Lady of the church is usually the subject of gossip.
Everything she does attracts comments from church members,
especially the women who use it as a subject for gossip:

*'Her dressing was too flamboyant for a First Lady.'
'Her make-up was inappropriate.'
'First Lady must be a little more fashionable –
she's too drab.'
'First Lady is too assertive. She should learn to be
in the background.'*

The gossips can go on and on. The question is, why should
you gossip about anybody, more so the First Lady? It is
ungodly. Repent if you find pleasure in gossiping about
your First Lady!

LADIES, WHY COMPETE WITH THE FIRST LADY OVER AN ALREADY-MARRIED PASTOR?

PROVERBS 5:3-23

*'For the lips of a strange woman drop as an
honeycomb, and her mouth is smoother than oil:
But her end is bitter as wormwood, sharp as a
two-edged sword.'* (KJV)

The ladies who are eyeing the First Lady position –
understand that the position has already been filled. Pastor
is already married, and will not be taking a second wife,

so what is the point in competing with First Lady? Or you are hoping Pastor will divorce his wife or do you pray that somehow First Lady will die so that you can steal your way into Pastor's life? Stop these unholy thoughts because these scenarios will not even happen. If you are ready for marriage, pray to get a single person just like you. It is sinful to be fantasising over someone else's husband.

WHY DO YOU WANT TO KNOW EVERYONE'S BUSINESS IN THE CHURCH?

2 THESSALONIANS 3:11

'We hear that some among you are idle and disruptive. They are not busy; they are busybodies.' (NIV)

Be friendly in church. Be approachable in church. Be concerned about church members. But do not make it your primary assignment to be poking your nose into everybody's private matters in church. Know your boundaries. Yes, you are concerned but do not use it as an excuse to dig into people's private lives. When you hear that a member has an issue, pray for them. It is not right for you to be nosing around issues that are none of your business. This attitude of some church members has led to a lot of strife and divisions in churches because it is the bedrock of gossip in the church.

DON'T TAKE UP ALL OF THE PASTOR'S TIME AFTER SERVICE; OTHERS ARE WAITING TO SEE HIM

PHILIPPIANS 2:3-8

'Don't be selfish; don't try to impress others. Be humble, thinking of others as better than

yourselves. Don't look out only for your own interests, but take an interest in others, too. You must have the same attitude that Christ Jesus had.' (NLT)

The pastor is a father for all. His doors are always open to everyone who wishes to see him, whether rich or poor, male or female. As a result, please, church member, when you get the opportunity to see the pastor do not spend too long there, especially on a Sunday. Understand that other people also need an opportunity to see the pastor. Be considerate. If you know that the issue you want to discuss with him will require a longer time, schedule a time within the week and see the pastor. By that time there may be fewer people at the office to see him.

CHURCH MEMBER, STOP SLEEPING DURING ALL-NIGHT SERVICES!

ACTS 20:9

'Seated in a window was a young man named Eutychus, who was sinking into a deep sleep as Paul talked on and on. When he was sound asleep, he fell to the ground from the third story and was picked up dead.' (NIV)

All night services are not for sleeping. Do not leave the comfort of your bed and go to an all-night service only to sleep. All-night services are for serious spiritual warfare. Nobody sleeps at the battlefront so why do you sleep at the all-night service? When you know you will attend a service, get adequate rest, and condition your mind for it. If possible, fast that day, and eat only some light food before the service. Heavy eating (especially carbohydrates and fats) will make you *easily* drowsy. The funny thing is that when a member is sleeping and you wake them up, they instantly start speaking in tongues, pretending to be in the Spirit. Stop pretending!

THOSE WHO DON'T FAST BUT PRETEND THEY ARE STARVING – YOUR CUP WILL BE FULL SOON

MATTHEW 6:16

'When you fast, do not look somber as the hypocrites do, for they disfigure their faces to show others they are fasting. Truly I tell you, they have received their reward in full.' (NIV)

When the pastor calls for fasting and prayers, some members pretend to be fasting, but they are not. They go around with sombre looks and pious countenance. But they are not fasting. Please fast when asked to do so. Corporate fasting is very necessary to battle certain issues confronting the church or nation. That is why all members have to participate fully so that the church can present a united front for spiritual battle. For those who realise they have a stomach ulcer, or have a hidden illness only when a fast is declared, may the Lord heal you.

YOU SPEND ONE HOUR ON YOUR MAKEUP, YET YOU COMPLAIN OF ONE-HOUR PRAYERS!

JAMES 4:8

'Come close to God, and God will come close to you. Wash your hands, you sinners; purify your

hearts, for your loyalty is divided between God and the world.' (NLT)

You are always complaining that prayer meetings take too long (even though they are just one hour)! But have you considered how long it takes for you to do your makeup? Some ladies can spend more than an hour on their makeup alone. Then they will spend an extra hour trying on new clothes and accessories. As a result, they always get to church late. Interestingly, these are the same people who complain that church has taken too long. They get angry that the prayer meetings are one hour long. 'It should be less.' You need to repent!

DO NOT LOOK FOR YOUR BIBLES ONLY ON SUNDAYS!

PSALM 119:105

'Your word is a lamp for my feet, a light on my path.' (NIV)

Church Member, spend time studying your Bible. Do not only look for it on Sundays. The Word of God should form the foundation of your daily Christian life. Have a personal Bible study plan, and develop the discipline to follow through with the plan. Your maturity in Christianity is measured by how well you know the Word of God, and how prepared you are to walk in the Word.

7

Young Worship Leader
and Choir Member

CHAPTER SEVEN

Young Worship Leader and Choir Member

STOP FAKING YOUR VOICE

MARK 14:26
*'And when they had sung a hymn,
they went out to the Mount of Olives.'* (NIV)

You have a beautiful natural voice, Worship Leader. Use it to bless God's people. Contemporary gospel musicians and worship leaders want to mimic their foreign counterparts, and therefore sing with some strange accent. There is nothing wrong with having a foreign gospel musician as a role model. But please, maintain your own voice. If you think it is hoarse, do more voice training and let it become suitable for your ministry. Honestly, it becomes irritating when you try to sing like someone you are not.

KNOW YOUR KEY BEFORE YOU GET ON STAGE

Knowing the key you are going to use to minister is a basic requirement every worship leader knows. Do not mount the stage before you start gesticulating to the instrumentalists. Let them know ahead of time so that they prepare for you. Furthermore, do not start singing and then hit a snag, before you retreat and use the key that is appropriate for the song you are ministering.

REMEMBER, THE STAGE IS AN ALTAR; NO MESSING ABOUT

Respect the stage you mount to minister. That stage carries the presence of God. Pastors stand on it to preach and pray. All kinds of prayers are offered on that stage. People kneel on that stage and pour out their heart to God. Angels of God have performed surgeries on that stage. So, when you get the privilege to stand on that stage to minister, show reverence to God. Before you minister, prepare yourself spiritually. You may decide to seek the face of God through fasting and prayer before mounting that stage. If there is any area of your life which does not please God, please work on it before getting on the stage. Some people have attracted curses on themselves because they disrespected the stage.

THE GOSSIP IS TOO MUCH IN THE CHOIR

It is now apparent that choirs are notoriously fertile places for gossip. Choristers congregate in some corner when they go for rehearsals and gossip about anybody they feel like gossiping about. They talk about the pastor, his wife, family, choir director, and who has a boyfriend and who does not. This attitude of the choir has predictably led to all the conflicts and bad blood that exist among choristers. In some choirs, there are divisions or competing gangs. Though they call themselves Christians, some choristers are not on talking terms due to the incessant gossip. The energy spent gossiping could be used to learn new songs and practice voice training. Choirs, please do everything you can to change this negative perception.

LEADING WORSHIP IS A SPIRITUAL EXERCISE SO AS YOU PREPARE YOUR SONGS, PRAY AS WELL!

Leading worship is not an act of entertainment. That is why you prepare extensively before you mount the stage to perform. Do all that you need to do: song selection, arrangement, choice of key and so on. But most importantly, pray and pray and pray. As you minister before the people of God, a lot of things happen in the spirit realm. Sicknesses are healed. Relationships are repaired. Deliverance takes place. As a result of all these, do not take worship as any other entertainment activity. It is a serious tool in the hands of God to visit His people. For you to flow in the will of God and allow the Holy Spirit to have His way, prepare yourself by prayer. You should also understand the fact that dark spiritual forces can impede your flow to prevent the people of God from being blessed. That is another reason why you ought to pray. Some years ago, I met a popular worship leader who suddenly lost her voice immediately she mounted the stage. For over 30 minutes nothing could come out of her vocal cords when she attempted to sing. When she went backstage, she regained her voice. The devil is fighting the worship of God. And Worship Leader, you are the first target!

DON'T LEAD WORSHIP TO IMPRESS OTHERS

Be careful that your worship will not be to impress the audience. Your assignment is not to impress anybody, not even the pastor or the church leadership. So do not sing songs that will win you applause. Do not sing just because you want to win an award. The craze for awards has caused many gospel musicians and worship leaders to stray from their calling. The only person whose award you should be concerned about is God Himself. Devote all your life working to impressing Him. Whatever you do on the stage should be directly aimed at impressing only the King.

WE WANT GOD'S PRESENCE; NOT ALL THESE GIMMICKS

Sometimes in leading worship, there is a temptation to employ a few gimmicks to excite your audience. It is a common sight these days to see worship leaders and praise team members employing all kinds of extraneous gesticulations in the course of the service or ministration, all aimed at getting the audience excited. But remember that it is God's presence we seek, not your gimmicks. If you are not careful you will end up exciting the audience but then lose the presence of God, which is the most important.

PLEASE DESIST FROM PLAYING TOO MANY SONGS DURING WORSHIP

In selecting and arranging your songs, be sure to focus on just a few songs. Choose the few that can communicate the presence of God during worship, instead of loading your song list. As you keep switching from one song to the other, the audience will lose the rhythm and miss the resultant spiritual connection. When you're ministering, be sensitive to the Spirit of God and keep singing the songs as and when you feel led. And please understand that worship is not just about songs, it could be in words as well. As you minister, take a pause and lead the congregation to pour out appellations to the Lord. It does not always have to be songs. Make proclamations as well.

REPORT TO PROGRAMMES EARLY AND STOP RUSHING TO MOUNT THE STAGE TO MINISTER

Going to church late is a mark of great disrespect to God. Going to minister late is equally a sign of disrespect to your ministry. You should not be late for your ministration, and then rush to the stage to lead when the programme has already started. It is necessary that you report to church early, and spend some time in prayer with your team before you go on stage to minister. Rushing onstage because you're late will make you commit even more errors.

DON'T THINK THAT YOU ARE INDISPENSABLE!

Worship Leader, you are not indispensable. Stop blackmailing everyone in the church, and holding church leadership to ransom. The practice where worship leaders refuse to perform because the pastor or a leader has offended them is unacceptable in the house of God. Understand that church will continue even when you drop dead. God always keeps a remnant, and He will raise a replacement if there is a need for it. There can never be a vacuum in God's house. So please see the opportunity to minister as a privilege. Cherish that privilege, and be thankful for it.

RAISE UP OTHER YOUNG WORSHIPPERS; YOU MIGHT NOT ALWAYS BE THERE

A key role you have to play as a worship leader is to mentor other young worshippers to fill your place one day. The number of people you can raise largely determines your success in ministry. Consider the mentoring of young talents as a way of consolidating your legacy in the worship ministry. Draw up a deliberate plan to train interested young people in the ministry of worship. You can start with the youth class, where you draw up a schedule and train them. The second level will be to give them exposure by offering them opportunities to minister at church and other programmes. A successful mentorship programme will project you as a generational leader.

YOU DON'T LIKE GOING FOR REHEARSALS BUT ALWAYS WANT TO LEAD WORSHIP

Members of the praise and worship team must be constantly rehearsing to sharpen their competence. It is during these rehearsals that new songs are learnt, mistakes are corrected, songs that would be ministered on church days are selected and arranged and leaders are chosen. How can you miss these rehearsals yet still insist on leading worship? Every member of the praise and worship team must show discipline by attending every rehearsal as much as possible. The worship leader must insist on attendance at every rehearsal, and also make it a general rule that you do not perform when you miss rehearsal.

STAY HUMBLE AT ALL TIMES

You cannot lead worship or be a member of the praise and worship team and be arrogant. In the presence of God, you can be nothing but humble. Lucifer, probably the greatest worship leader in history (before he fell), lost his position because he exalted himself above the Elohim Himself. As a worship leader, the most important lesson you should never forget is that worship can only be acceptable to God in an atmosphere of humility. Being puffed up will only lead to your eventual downfall from grace. Whenever you feel arrogant, just consider what happened to the greatest worship leader and stay humble.

Printed in Great Britain
by Amazon

41512952R00064